LOOK UP WITH ME

NEIL deGRASSE TYSON:
A Life Among the Stars

By
JENNIFER BERNE

Illustrations by
LORRAINE NAM

With an introduction by
NEIL deGRASSE TYSON

Katherine Tegen Books
An Imprint of HarperCollinsPublishers

*To our ancient ancestor, the first animal who ever
looked up and wondered.*
—J.B.

To my omma and appa, who inspire me to keep looking up.
—L.N.

Katherine Tegen Books is an imprint of HarperCollins Publishers.

Look Up with Me: Neil deGrasse Tyson: A Life Among the Stars
Text copyright © 2019 by Jennifer Berne
Introduction copyright © 2019 by Neil deGrasse Tyson
Illustrations copyright © 2019 by Lorraine Nam
All rights reserved. Manufactured in China.
No part of this book may be used or reproduced in any manner whatsoever without written permission except in the case of brief quotations embodied in critical articles and reviews. For information address HarperCollins Children's Books, a division of HarperCollins Publishers, 195 Broadway, New York, NY 10007.
www.harpercollinschildrens.com

Library of Congress Cataloging-in-Publication Data
Names: Berne, Jennifer, author. | Nam, Lorraine, illustrator.
Title: Look up with me : Neil deGrasse Tyson : a life among the stars /
    words by Jennifer Berne ; illustrations by Lorraine Nam ; with an introduction by
    Neil deGrasse Tyson.
Other titles: Neil deGrasse Tyson : a life among the stars
Description: New York : Katherine Tegen Books, An Imprint of HarperCollins
    Publishers, [2019] | Audience: Age 4–8. | Audience: K to grade 3.
Identifiers: LCCN 2018021527 | ISBN 9780062844941 (hardback) |
    ISBN 9780062844958 (pbk.)
Subjects: LCSH: Tyson, Neil deGrasse. | Astrophysicists—United States—
    Biography. | Astronomy—Juvenile literature.
Classification: LCC QB460.72.T97 B47 2019 | DDC 520.92 [B]—dc23 LC record
    available at https://lccn.loc.gov/2018021527

The artist used paper, glue, colored pencils, a camera, and Adobe Photoshop to
create the illustrations for this book.
Typography by Aurora Parlagreco
22 23 SCP 10 9 8 7 6 5 4
❖
First Edition

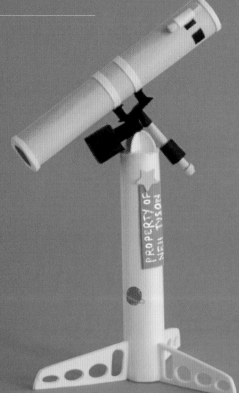

INTRODUCTION

Most grown-ups have forgotten what it was like to be a kid. Some don't remember on purpose—hurrying life along as fast as they can. For others, memories of being a kid simply faded from view.

I'm a full-grown grown-up. In fact, I'm so grown up that I have grown-up kids of my own. But I still feel like a kid. I've felt like a kid my entire life. Why? Because I'm a scientist. Scientists are kids who never lost their natural childhood curiosity about the world. Kids who lose that curiosity (usually around middle school) become normal adults. But kids who retain that curiosity eventually become scientists, either in their hearts or in their professions.

So even as you grow older, never stop being a kid. This will guarantee that the world—even the universe itself—becomes and remains your playground of curiosity.

Neil deGrasse Tyson
Astrophysicist, New York City

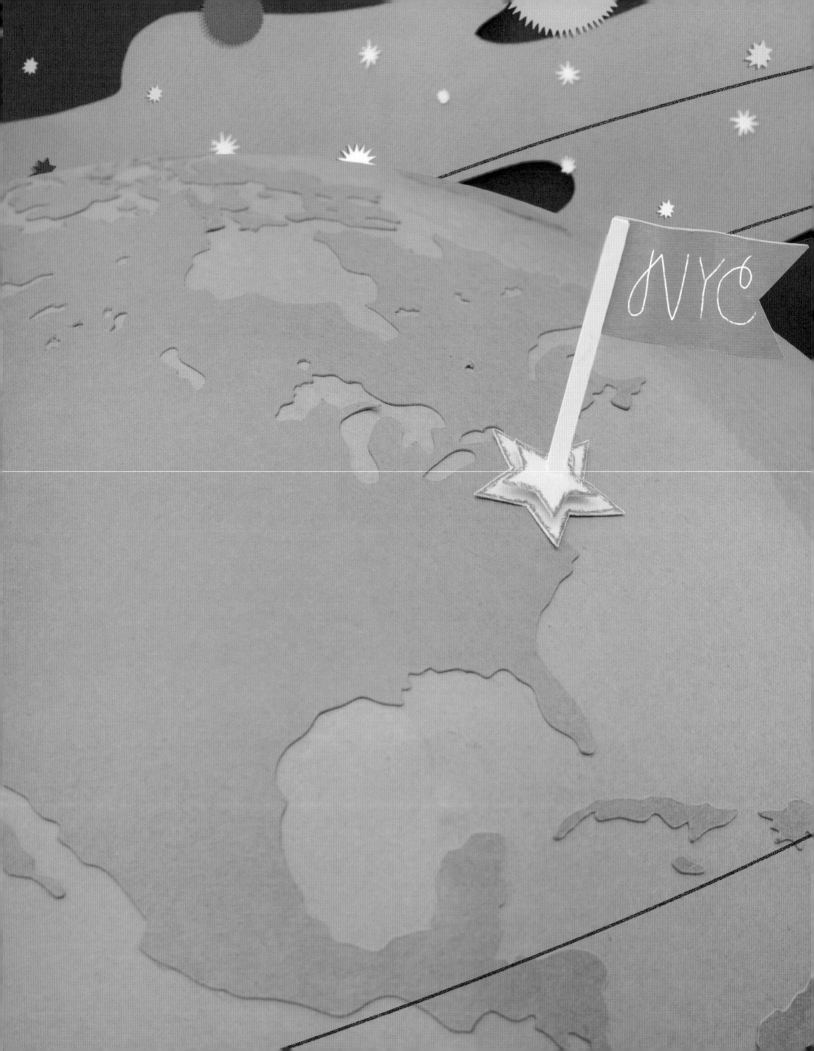

On an autumn afternoon in 1958,
in the city of New York,
on the third planet out from the Sun,
in the Milky Way galaxy,
a little baby boy was born.

Neil deGrasse Tyson opened his eyes,
and there it was.
The universe.
Just waiting to be discovered.

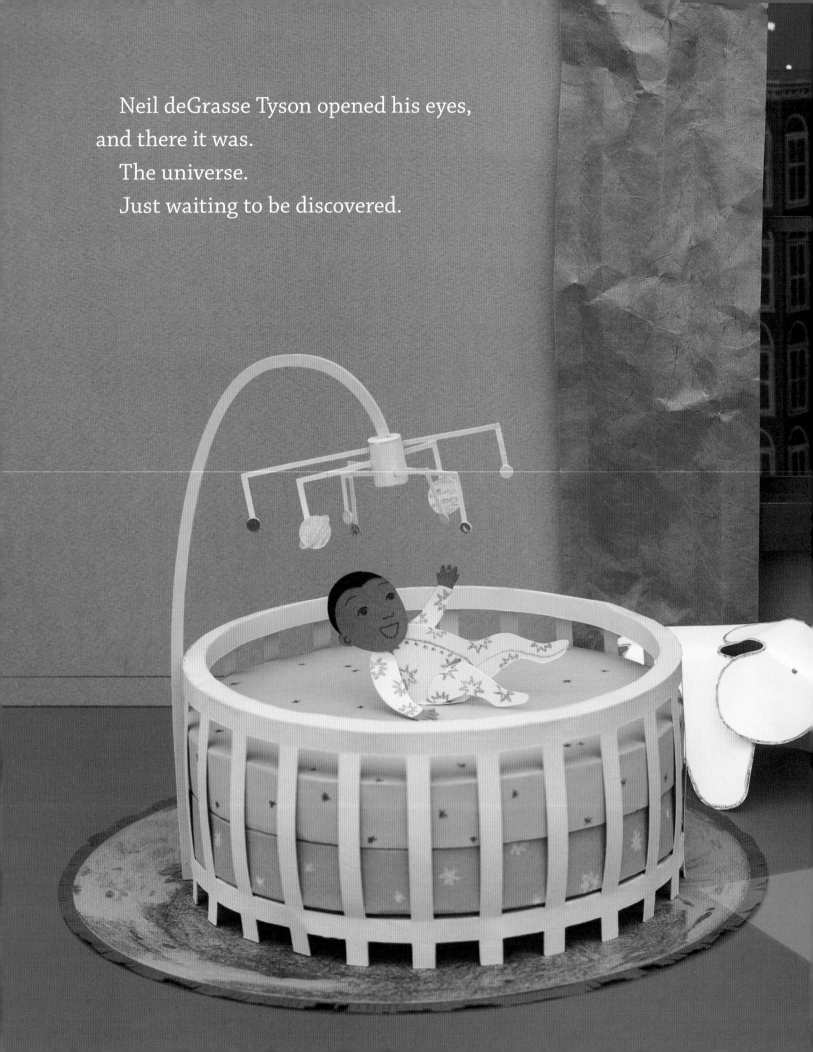

At first, Neil's world was small.
His building blocks and little
books. His yo-yos and gyroscopes.
During the days, Neil went
to school, to the park, and to
museums.

At night, he looked out the window of his apartment building and saw other buildings, streets and streetlights, and—here and there—small bits of sky.

Until . . .

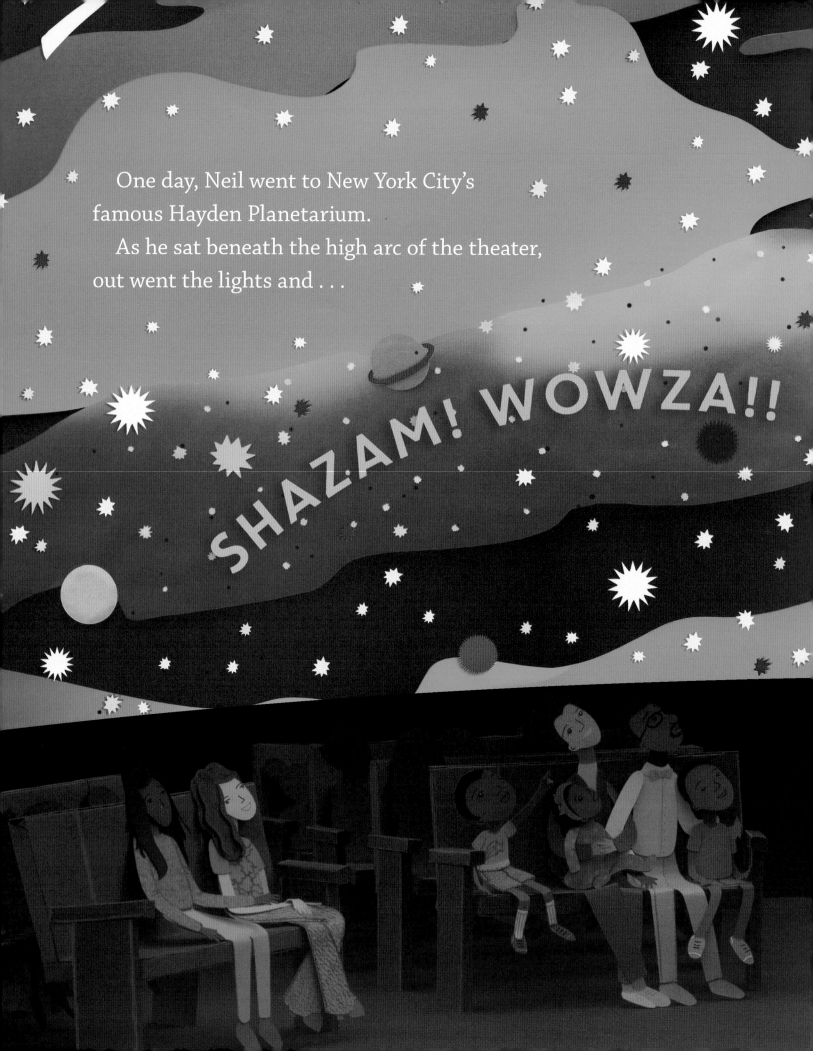

One day, Neil went to New York City's
famous Hayden Planetarium.
   As he sat beneath the high arc of the theater,
out went the lights and . . .

SHAZAM! WOWZA!!

Neil's mind was launched . . . into outer space!
In a single instant, his world expanded a hundred
times, a thousand times, even more.

Projected on the huge dome above his head was the
night sky with countless thousands of stars.
A gigantic, spectacular, beautiful cosmos Neil never
knew existed.
And in that moment, his life was changed forever.

Neil started reading everything he could about planets, moons, and stars.

He wondered where comets come from. What makes galaxies spin? And how big is outer space?

He learned the word "astrophysicist"—the kind of scientist who studies all those things—the kind of scientist he wanted to become someday.

Neil pasted glow-in-the-dark stars all over his ceiling in the shapes of the constellations. At night, with the lights out, it felt as though his bed were floating in the huge magnificence of space.

After exploring the skies with binoculars and a small telescope, Neil was determined to get a bigger, more powerful telescope. To bring the heavens even closer to his eyes.

And he figured out just how to do it.

Dogs!

For two entire years after school, Neil walked
neighborhood dogs.

Big ones,
    small ones,
        fluffy ones,
            scruffy ones.

At fifty cents a walk, he
worked hard and finally got his
telescope!

Night after night, Neil carried his heavy
telescope up to the roof of his building.
   Nervous neighbors called the police to report
a tall burglar with a dangerous weapon.

When the officers arrived, Neil explained it was a telescope and showed them the beauty of his favorite planet, Saturn, magnified one hundred times. Its golden glow. Its icy rings and many moons.

So, although they arrived with fear and suspicion, they left with awe and wonder.

Because of his passion for astronomy, Neil won a scholarship for a voyage across the Atlantic Ocean to view a total solar eclipse. Surrounded by stargazers, researchers, and scientists, Neil was beginning to find his people, his future.

Then, at only fifteen, Neil was invited to give his first astronomy lecture. He was paid fifty dollars—which equaled one hundred dog walks—and made him realize he could actually make a living by talking about the universe he loved so much.

In college and graduate school, Neil's mind traveled farther than it ever had before . . . flying into outer space with runaway stars, diving into the cores of black holes, and leaping from galaxy to galaxy.

And when Neil wasn't being his cosmic self, he enjoyed being his dancing self, his wrestling self, his picture-taking self. Or, most of all, his laughing self.

When Neil graduated, he made sharing the wonders of
the cosmos his world. As a teacher, a researcher, a writer.

He wrote a magazine column in the made-up character of Merlin, a five-billion-year-old visitor from the Andromeda galaxy who answered people's questions about astronomy and the cosmos.

Then Neil got what just might be the coolest job on Earth. He became . . .

. . . the director of the Hayden Planetarium.

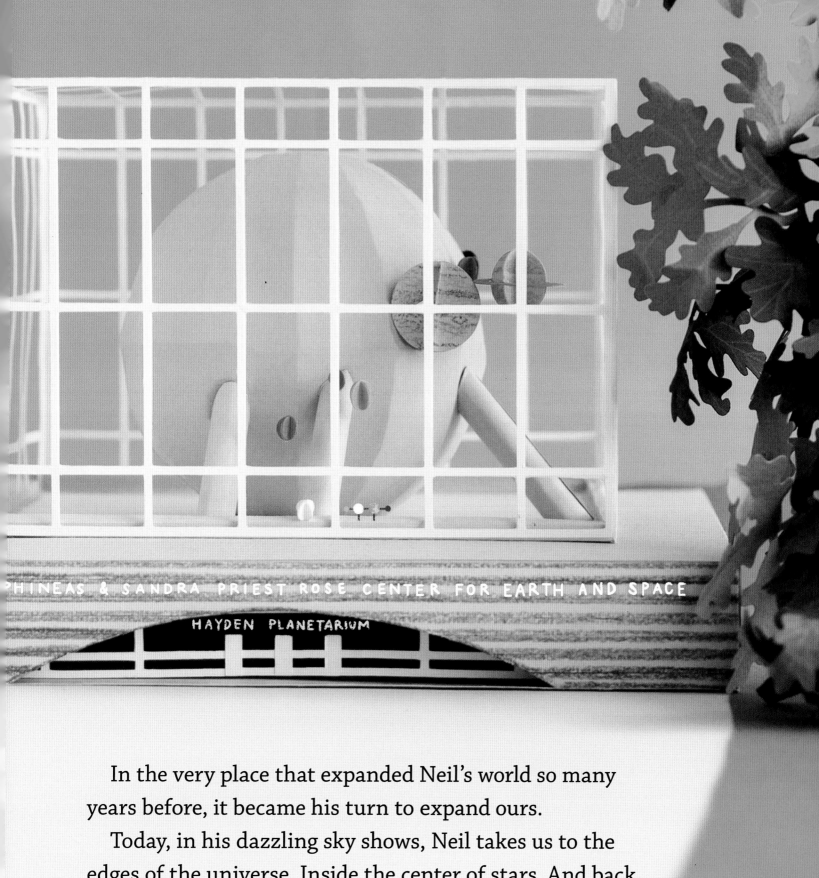

PHINEAS & SANDRA PRIEST ROSE CENTER FOR EARTH AND SPACE

HAYDEN PLANETARIUM

In the very place that expanded Neil's world so many years before, it became his turn to expand ours.

Today, in his dazzling sky shows, Neil takes us to the edges of the universe. Inside the center of stars. And back to the beginning of time.

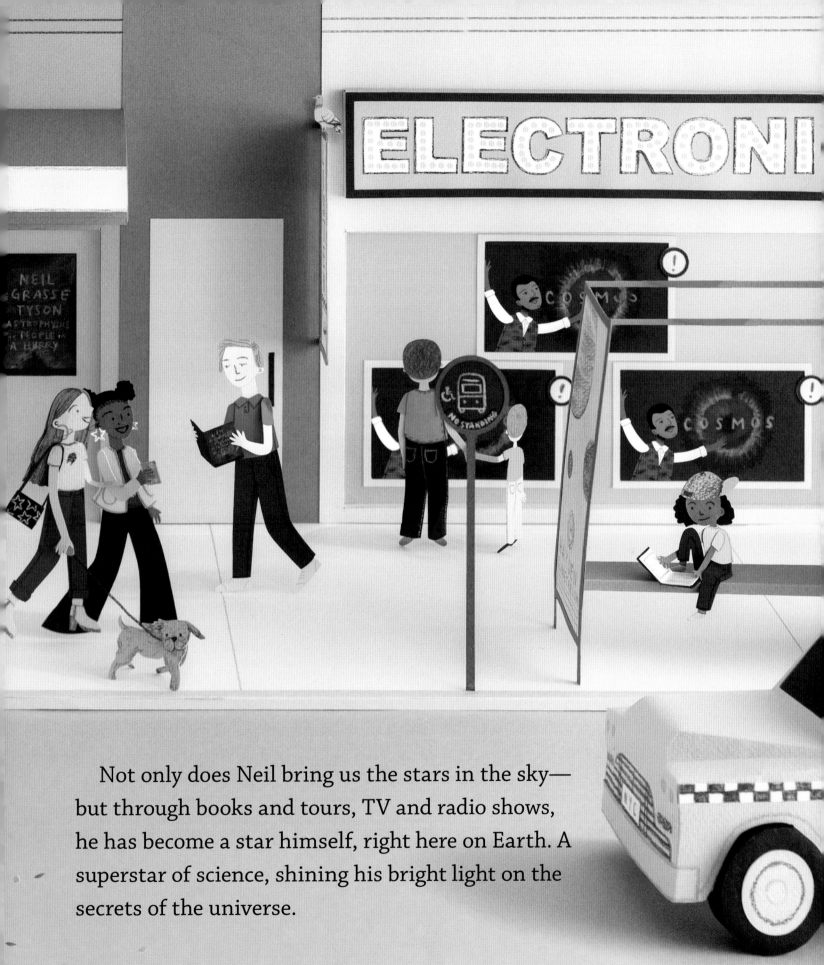

Not only does Neil bring us the stars in the sky—
but through books and tours, TV and radio shows,
he has become a star himself, right here on Earth. A
superstar of science, shining his bright light on the
secrets of the universe.

Neil believes everyone should have their mind blown at least once a day. And he does his best to make sure that happens.

There are more stars in the universe than grains of sand on all the beaches in the world.

Black holes may contain whole other universes.

If you get close to a black hole, your body will be sucked into it and stretched and stretched and stretched as you disappear into its depths which is called being "spaghettified"

"Shooting stars" are really meteors entering Earth's atmosphere. And most of them are smaller than a blueberry!

StarTalk
RADIO SHOW
WITH NEIL DEGRASSE TYSON

If Earth didn't have an atmosphere to scatter the sunlight,
the daytime sky would be as black as night.

Outer space is completely silent.
Because there's no air there,
it has nothing for sound to travel through.
Someone could shout right in your ear
and you wouldn't hear a thing.

$E = mc^2$

Neutron stars are the densest stars in the universe.
They are so dense that one teaspoon of a neutron star
would weigh more than twenty million elephants.

In five billion years, the sun will expand
and grow so large that it will engulf
Earth and all the planets in the solar system.

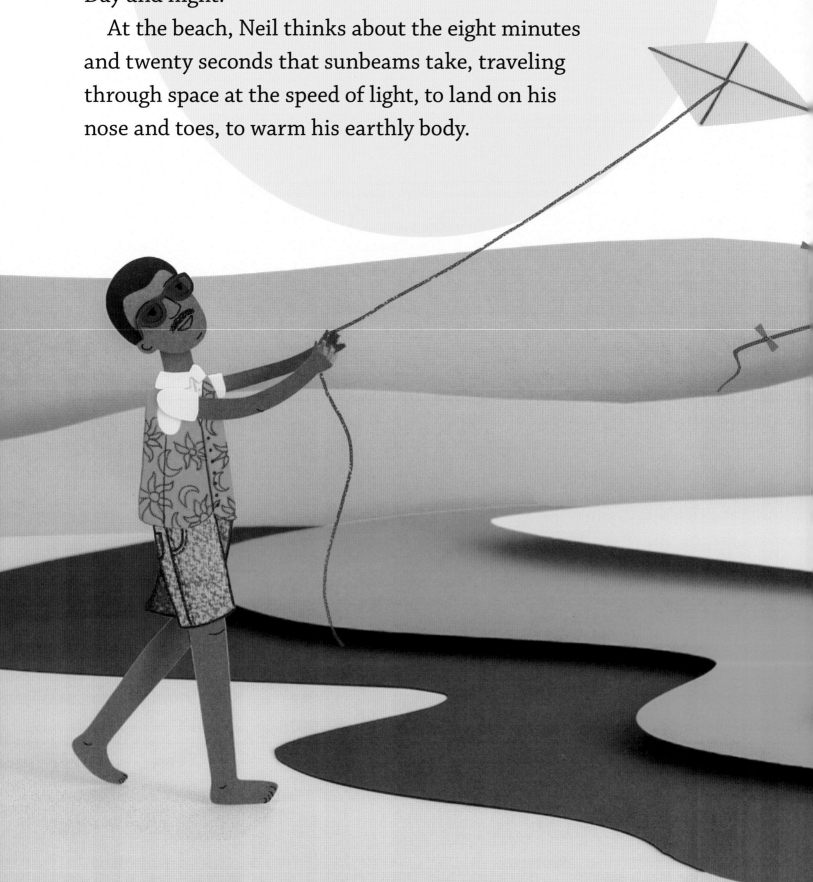

The wonders of the universe are always with Neil.
Day and night.

At the beach, Neil thinks about the eight minutes
and twenty seconds that sunbeams take, traveling
through space at the speed of light, to land on his
nose and toes, to warm his earthly body.

When Neil sees stars through his window at night, he thinks about how their light took thousands of years to get here. And that there are newborn stars whose light won't get to Earth for a thousand or more years into the future. Invisible stars, for now. Then he closes his eyes and goes to sleep in his beloved cosmos.

As much as Neil loves the amazing facts of the universe, he is also fascinated by the mysteries and the unknowns. The just-beginning-to-be-knowns and the barely-knowns.

The mysterious pull of invisible dark matter.

The push of dark energy, expanding our universe, ever larger, ever faster.

And wormholes . . . the faster-than-light passageways through space and through time.

All the mind-blowing secrets that will be explored by the next generation of scientists and the next.

Perhaps by you.

One simple wish Neil has for the future is that
all of us, every person on Earth, go outside at night
and look up, look up, look up . . .

At the moon, stars, and planets.

And think about the fact that we are made of the very same stuff they are—of the stardust atoms of long-ago exploded stars.

And that we're all part of the very same thing— this amazing, beautiful, spectacular, mind-blowing universe that is our home.

That is our world.

That is us.

AUTHOR'S NOTE

Twelve years ago, when I was just beginning my book-writing career, I sent a package to one of my inspirational heroes, Neil deGrasse Tyson. In it were three of my newly written manuscripts—stories about the sea, our planet, and the cosmos.

A few weeks later, I received an envelope from the Hayden Planetarium. I was thrilled. A response from Neil! His letter thanked me for sharing my passions with him and was wonderfully encouraging and complimentary about my concepts and my writing. At the same time, he was cautiously realistic, asking, "Have you collected your forty rejection letters yet? I don't know why, but it seems to be a rite of passage." He said he saw no reason why I wouldn't get published. And then he ended by saying, "Good luck in your continued efforts to bring the universe down to earth."

Well, he was right. I did get my stories published—but not without collecting a folder of rejection letters first. I persisted, and it paid off. Ever since, I've been sharing my passions in my books, writing about the amazing universe and the people who discover its secrets.

Then, in 2017, in a wonderful turn of events, things began to come full circle. HarperCollins publisher Katherine Tegen and editor Mabel Hsu had read my books about Jacques Cousteau and Albert Einstein, and they were planning a new picture book biography of Neil deGrasse Tyson. They wondered if I would be willing to write it. I couldn't say yes fast enough!

What an incredible opportunity to spend months doing research on my inspirational hero and then write this book. So now it's my turn to encourage all of you to follow your curiosity and share your passions. And to persevere through your rejections, which will almost surely be followed by your successes.

We live on an amazing planet, in an astounding universe, with so much to discover and share with each other. Keep seeking the truth and following your passions!

GLOSSARY

ANDROMEDA GALAXY
A spiral galaxy that is approximately 2.5 million light-years from Earth. It is the nearest galaxy to our own Milky Way galaxy.

ASTROPHYSICIST
A scientist who studies the physical laws and behavior of stars, planets, all natural objects in space, and the workings of the universe.

ATOM
A building block for all things in the universe. All things are made of chemicals, and chemicals are made of atoms. An atom is the smallest part of any chemical element that still retains the characteristics of that element.

BLACK HOLE
A region of space with such intense gravity that nothing—no matter, no light—can escape it.

COMET
A ball of frozen gases, rock, and dust that orbits the Sun. Jets of gas and dust from comets form long tails that can be seen from Earth.

CONSTELLATION
A group of stars forming a recognizable pattern, traditionally named after creatures and people from mythology.

COSMOS
The universe, seen as an orderly and harmonious system.

DARK ENERGY
A mysterious invisible pressure that pushes outward and causes the universe to expand at an ever-accelerating rate.

DARK MATTER
An invisible force whose source cannot be directly observed but exerts a gravitational pull on all other matter around it . . . a force so strong it holds galaxies together.

GALAXY
A system of millions, sometimes billions of stars, together with gases and dust, held together by gravity. Some galaxies are spiral shaped, others are oval shaped (called "elliptical"), and others are irregular shapes. Scientists estimate that there may be as many as one hundred billion galaxies in the observable universe.

GRAVITY
A force of attraction—pulling objects toward each other—that exists between any two masses, any two particles. This attraction exists between all objects, everywhere in the universe. The more massive the object, the greater its gravitational pull.

LIGHT-YEAR
A unit for measuring very large astronomical distances. A light-year is the distance that light would travel in one year. The speed of light is 186,282 miles per second. So in one year light travels almost six trillion miles.

METEOR
A pebble-size fragment of a comet or asteroid streaking through Earth's upper atmosphere. Air friction causes these objects to glow and vaporize.

MILKY WAY GALAXY
The galaxy that contains our solar system. Besides our Sun and its planets, the Milky Way contains between 200 billion and 400 billion stars. It is called "milky" because from Earth the light shining from that many stars blurs together, causing a white, milky appearance.

PLANETARIUM
A theater in which images of stars, planets, and constellations are projected on the inside of a dome-shaped ceiling, combined with commentary and video effects, for entertainment and education.

RUNAWAY STAR
A star moving through space at an unusually fast speed. Thought to be the result of an explosion of a nearby star that caused the runaway star to be flung into space at super-high speed.

SOLAR SYSTEM
A star together with all the objects and planets that revolve around it. Our solar system consists of the Sun (our star) in the center; eight planets and their moons; dozens of dwarf planets; millions of asteroids, meteoroids, and comets; and countless particles of smaller debris.

SPEED OF LIGHT
The speed light travels, as measured in a vacuum (a space where there is no matter or pressure). That speed is 186,282 miles per second. It is believed that nothing in the universe is physically able to travel faster than the speed of light.

STAR
A huge glowing ball of hot gas held together by gravity. Stars produce light and energy by a powerful compression process called nuclear fusion. When this happens, a tremendous amount of energy is released, causing the star's core to heat up to temperatures ranging from 10,000 to 200 million degrees Fahrenheit.

SUN
Our Sun is at the center of our solar system. It is about 4.6 billion years old, and so big that about one million Earths could fit inside it. Temperatures inside the Sun's core can reach 27 million degrees Fahrenheit.

UNIVERSE
All of space and everything in it. Everything that exists. The universe has been expanding since its creation, in what is called the "Big Bang," about 13 billion years ago.

WORMHOLE
A wormhole is a theoretical passageway, like a tunnel, through space and time, that could create shortcuts for traveling across the universe.

HOW TO HAVE MORE NEIL DEGRASSE TYSON IN YOUR LIFE

BOOKS

You can find Neil's complete list of books at www.haydenplanetarium.org/tyson/buy/books. Here are a few of my favorites.

Merlin's Tour of the Universe: A Skywatcher's Guide to Everything from Mars and Quasars to Comets, Planets, Blue Moons, and Werewolves. New York: Doubleday, 1997.

The Sky Is Not the Limit: Adventures of an Urban Astrophysicist. Amherst, NY: Prometheus Books, 2004.

Death by Black Hole: And Other Cosmic Quandaries. New York: W. W. Norton & Company, 2007.

(with Donald Goldsmith). *Origins: Fourteen Billion Years of Cosmic Evolution.* New York: W. W. Norton & Company, 2014.

Astrophysics for People in a Hurry. New York: W. W. Norton & Company, 2017.

ONLINE

Neil deGrasse Tyson at the Hayden Planetarium website: www.haydenplanetarium.org/tyson

Past and present *StarTalk* radio episodes: www.startalkradio.net

On Facebook: www.facebook.com/neildegrassetyson

On Twitter: www.twitter.com/neiltyson

IN PERSON

At the Hayden Planetarium: www.amnh.org/our-research/hayden-planetarium

On tour: www.haydenplanetarium.org/tyson/upcoming-appearances

HOW TO HAVE MORE UNIVERSE IN YOUR LIFE

BOOKS

There are thousands of books about all aspects of the universe. Aside from the ones written by Neil, here are a few about the cosmos.

Aguilar, David A. *Planets, Stars, and Galaxies: A Visual Encyclopedia of Our Universe.* Washington, DC: National Geographic, 2002.

DK, *Space!* New York: DK Publishing, 2015.

Driscoll, Michael, and Meredith Hamilton. *A Child's Introduction to the Night Sky: The Story of the Stars, Planets and Constellations—and How You Can Find Them in the Sky.* New York: Black Dog & Leventhal, 2004.

ONLINE

The Hayden Planetarium and the American Museum of Natural History: www.amnh.org

NASA: www.nasa.gov

NASA: Imagine the Universe!: www.imagine.gsfc.nasa.gov

Space.com: www.space.com

HubbleSite: www.hubblesite.org

The Universe at History.com: www.history.com/shows/the-universe

BBC Space: www.bbc.co.uk/science/space

IN PERSON

You're in it. The universe is everything, everywhere. Just be curious and observant. And ask questions.

There are many excellent museums and planetariums all over the country and the world with fascinating exhibits and information about our planet and our universe. Remember, that's how Neil first got inspired!

If you want more of the cosmos, you too can earn money to buy a small telescope and start studying the night sky. Some telescopes even come with camera attachments. Neil had one of those when he was young and took pictures he still loves and treasures today.